Inhalt English – Sprachkurs 2

1	Boston | Plymouth	
2	Boston | Harvard	5
3	Boston | Boston Tea Party	7
4	National Parks | Yosemite	9
5	National Parks | Bryce Canyon	10
6	National Parks | Grand Canyon	12
7	San Francisco | Chinatown	13
8	San Francisco | Golden Gate Bridge	15
9	San Francisco | An argument	16
10	Atlanta | Olympic Games	18
11	Atlanta | Shopping mall	20
12	Atlanta | Airport	22
13	Atlanta | Car rental	23
14	Chicago | Art Institute	25
15	Chicago | Symphony Orchestra	27
16	Chicago | Futures market	28
17	Washington | World Bank	30
18	Washington | Hospital	32
19	Washington | At the hairdresser's	33
20	Orlando | Gossip on the beach	34
21	Orlando | Fast-food restaurant	36
22	Orlando | Cape Canaveral	38
23	New York | Little Italy	39
24	New York | Wall Street	40
25	New York | 5th Avenue	42
26	New York | Jewish synagogue	44
27	Los Angeles | In the office	45
28	Los Angeles | Silicon Valley	47
29	Los Angeles | Rodeo Drive	49

1 Boston | Plymouth

Den Jahrestag der Landung der Mayflower in Plymouth erleben Adam und Mary in historischen Kostümen der Pilger. Mary möchte ernsthaft mit ihrem Mann über ihre Beziehung reden, doch Adam nutzt seine Verkleidung zu Späßen!

- What are your plans?

- We have the possibility to build a new life together here in New England. You can make me your husband in three months and have three children, one next year in 1621, one in 1623 and one in 1625.

- Adam, I am your wife and we're in the 1990's and I'm talking to you seriously. What plans do you have concerning jobs?

- I am thinking about developing the ship-building industry in Plymouth with a group of friends. These are hard times but we are making sacrifices.

- What are you talking about?

- We are putting our heads together to get ideas and not to make the same mistakes as in England. William is planning to do something in textiles and I want to build modern ships like the Mayflower.

- You're not giving me a straight answer.

- What's wrong? Now we're living this side of the Atlantic, we are starting to organize our new life.

- I'm tired, I want to sit down, and I'm not in the mood to listen to this. I just want to know when you're changing jobs.

- I want to have a job where I'm miles away from you, that's all.

- Ha, ha. Make an effort to please me today for once. It's our special day and we're having dinner somewhere nice tonight, so phone Madeleine to ask her to babysit for us tonight.

- OK. Steve is coming with us. He's really nice.

- What!? This is our romantic evening, just the two of us!

- All good things are three!

possibility: Möglichkeit
seriously: ernsthaft
concerning: bezüglich
to develop: aufbauen
sacrifice: Opfer
straight answer: vernünftige Antwort
mood: Laune

2 Boston | Harvard

Ein paar Freunde sitzen auf dem Campus der renommierten 'Harvard University'. Doch ihr Gespräch ist nicht so intellektuell, wie man es von den Studenten erwarten würde.

- I want another pizza.

- What? How many pizzas are you going to eat?

- You eat like a horse!

- Be careful, you're going to get fat one day.

- No I'm not. But I need sustenance. How do you expect me to think and develop my mind if I don't have enough food? An outstanding academic record demands a lot of energy.

- Who do you think you are, Einstein?

- No, but let's face it, we are the elite of America.

- Ah, come off it!

- This place was founded in 1636 and has seen the greatest people pass through here since then. Theodore and Franklin D. Roosevelt were here for instance, and JFK.

- It doesn't mean you have to pig out on pizza all the time.

- It's a free country, and if I want another pizza, I'll have one.

- Well I'm not having any more. I have to watch my weight.

- 🟥 **You're fishing for compliments.** You just want everyone to say what a nice body you have and how beautiful you are.

- 🟨 Well at least it's true, and I'm prepared to make compliments as long as they're true.

- 🟥 You just like having lots of women around you. **You've got a one-track mind.** But it's not by being **slimy** that you're going to get anyone.

- 🟨 He's not slimy, he's galant and charming as well as **hunky** and manly.

- 🟥 Right, well you both seem to have found the right person!

- 🟨 Yeah, George is a real cutie!

- 🟨 Give us a kiss.

- 🟥 God, this is sickening!

- 🟨 If you played more sports instead of reading, you'd have nice muscly arms like this.

- 🟥 Don't tell me you only go for the inner qualities.

- 🟥 Not only, of course not. Anyway, I'm getting a pizza.

- 🟨 Actually, if you're getting one, perhaps I'll have one too!

---

to eat like a horse: essen wie ein Scheunendrescher
to get fat: dick werden
sustenance: Nahrung
academic record: akademische Leistung
let's face it: sehen wir den Tatsachen ins Auge
to pig out: sich voll stopfen
to be fishing for compliments: auf Komplimente aus sein
to have a one-track mind: immer nur eine Sache im Kopf haben
slimy: schleimig
hunky: gut gebaut

3 Boston | Boston Tea Party

Am 16. Dezember 1773 warfen die Bewohner Bostons ganze Schiffsladungen voll Tee ins Hafenbecken. Im folgenden Gespräch erfährt man einiges über die Hintergründe der Boston Tea Party.

- It was on December 16th, 1773 that people threw whole shiploads of tea into the harbor.

- Why exactly did they do that?

- It was to protest against the taxes and the complete ban the British had imposed on trade with other countries.

- What did that achieve?

- I don't know what the immediate effect of it was. But the delegates of all the colonies except Georgia met in Philadelphia and agreed to break off all trade relations with Britain.

- I guess it's famous because it represented a deterioration in relations.

- And from then on there was no stopping the anti-British feeling.

- Was there any point where the British were on the verge of winning in the War of Independence?

- They won some battles, but perhaps it was inevitable that they would lose in the end.

- Washington received the support of the French as well, didn't he?

- Yes. France recognized the independence of the thirteen colonies and fought alongside them.

- And, later, the leaders of the French Revolution got a lot of their ideas from the Americans.

- Boston was a center of revolutionary activity. At that time it was one of the largest towns here, but not any more of course.

- No, it's nothing compared to New York, L.A. or Chicago. It's hard to imagine living in those days.

- It must have been fun chucking all that tea into the water!

- I don't even like tea, so I certainly wouldn't have minded.

- Don't you ever drink tea?
- Only at Chinese restaurants sometimes. What do you think about Anglo-American relations nowadays?
- Well, they're very good because of the historic links, the language, where people come from ...
- History has actually brought them close together.
- Well, the English like to talk about the 'special relationship' they think they have with the US. But obviously the English have interests elsewhere just like the Americans.
- I think the past is more or less irrelevant. You have to look forward.
- Yep. This is the age of international unions and organizations and agreements.
- Do you think that will make things better?
- Well, the Brits, for example, are still often a little bit reserved about the EU. But all these unions can only be a step in the right direction.

---

harbor: Hafen
tax: Steuer
ban: Verbot
to achieve: erreichen
trade relations: Handelsbeziehungen
deterioration: Verschlechterung
to be on the verge of sth: kurz vor etw. stehen
compared to: im Vergleich zu
to chuck: schmeißen
nowadays: heutzutage
link: Verbindung
obviously: offensichtlich
union: Staatenbund

4 National Parks | Yosemite

Bei einer Tour im Yosemite Nationalpark lernen sich zwei Wanderer kennen. Tony kennt sich in der Umgebung sehr gut aus und gibt sein Wissen an Stacey weiter. Es gibt wirklich eine Menge über Yosemite zu erfahren!

- I've just seen Mono Lake, which isn't far from here.

- Oh yeah, it's beautiful. An alkaline lake of volcanic origin.

- You're a bit of an expert, are you?

- No, just a bit of a show-off!

- Apparently, the whole ecosystem of the lake is threatened by the water consumption of L.A. and the surroundings.

- I hope it won't be destroyed.

- This water problem exists in quite a few states. It's become a valuable product. Can you tell me something about Yosemite?

- Sure. I come here almost every year. It's a fantastic place in all seasons. You can visit Yosemite Valley all year, although Tioga Road through the High Sierra is closed in winter.

- They told me to reserve accommodation a long time in advance, especially for between June and September.

- Well it's extremely popular. I think over 4 million visitors come here every year. They want to see the chipmunks and the bears, the two hundred species of bird, the reptiles.

- And I know a lot go free climbing here.

- Yes, especially up the Half Dome and El Capitán on the west corner. It's called the Half Dome because of its shape obviously.

- And that's El Capitán there, isn't it?

- That's right. What made you decide to come here?

- There's a famous photographer called Ansel Adams who took breathtaking pictures of this national park. I then wanted to capture the spirit of the place myself and see

- the granite rock faces and the nearly vertical waterfalls with my own eyes.
- Have you seen the redwoods in Mariposa Grove?
- Yeah. They're amazing! It's hard to believe trees can grow to that height.
- There's one which is 64 metres high, 9 metres in diameter at the base of the trunk and has two-meter-thick branches! Not surprisingly, it's called the Giant Grizzly. Yosemite is the Indian word for the grizzly bear. Did you know that?
- No I didn't. But I've seen one.
- Here?
- No, in a zoo once!
- It's quite an impressive animal.
- One swipe of its paw and you're gone!

---

alkaline: alkalisch
show-off: Angeber
threatened: gefährdet
surroundings: Umgebung
to destroy: zerstören
valuable: wertvoll
accommodation: Unterkunft
chipmunk: Backenhörnchen
to capture sth: etw. einfangen
rock face: Felswand
redwood: Mammutbaum
diameter: Durchmesser

5 National Parks | Bryce Canyon

Steve und Jane wandern durch den Bryce Canyon und erzählen, was so besonders an ihm ist. Aber sie sollten vorsichtig sein – laut indianischer Legenden erwachen die Geister bei zu viel Lärm!

- Phew! I'm hot!
- So am I. Let's have a drink.
- Well, it's hot now, but it's supposed to get very cool at night.
- It's something like two and a half thousand meters above sea level.
- Look at these strange semicircular bays.

- I suppose it's the erosion that does that.
- It's funny how nature creates all these spectacular shapes.
- Yes. You talk of the seven wonders of the world but there are hundreds of natural and man-made wonders in the world.
- I think it would be difficult for me to pick out the best seven!
- Anyway, this is definitely wonderful!
- It's worth the effort.
- Well it wasn't that much of an effort. We did take the Navajo Trail, which is only 2.2 miles long.
- Yes, it's a good deal shorter than the Rim Trail or Peekaboo Trail. They're 5.5 miles long.
- That's not too far either, is it?
- I'm not very fit at the moment, I know, but it's because of the heat as well.
- But the short trails are enough just to get a good quick view of the landscape.
- Ooooohhh!!
- Sshh! You're not supposed to shout like that! You'll wake up the old Indian spirits.
- Oh, don't talk crap!
- Come on, keep going!
- I like the pinky-red color of the landscape here.
- Yeah, it's lovely.
- I think you're going to turn more than pinky-red!
- Never mind that! Who was Bryce anyway?
- I read he tried to raise cattle here.
- Maybe he was one of the Mormons. They were the first white settlers here.
- I don't know. But I know his forename was Ebenezer. Awful name, don't you think?

---

it's supposed to: es soll
sea level: Meeresspiegel
semicircular: halbrund
bay: Bucht
to be worth the effort: der Mühe wert sein
trail: Wanderweg
to talk crap: Quatsch reden
to raise cattle: Vieh züchten
settler: Siedler

6 National Parks | Grand Canyon

Es heißt, der Grand Canyon sei die größte und schönste Schlucht der Welt. Ein Ranger gibt einer Touristin ausführliche Informationen, damit sie nichts verpasst.

- Have tourists been coming here for a long time?

- The first hotel was built at Grand View Point in 1892. And it was founded as a national park in 1919. People have been coming here ever since.

- How long have you been a park ranger?

- I've been doing this job for over ten years now.

- And you don't get tired of it?

- Tired? Not really. Well, of course, every job has its routine.

- But where are you going to get scenery like this and be able to admire it every day?

- It gets too hot in the middle of the summer. That's one drawback.

- How big is it?

- In miles or kilometers?

- Kilometers, it's more normal for me.

- Four thousand nine hundred and thirty four square kilometers. That's larger than Yosemite and much bigger than Bryce Canyon.

- You couldn't fit too many of these in Europe! Do you ever have any major problems? Do accidents happen?

- No, just the odd sprained ankle, of course, like anywhere! But when people go off on their own, they sometimes overdo it a little bit. And you have to be careful. This is rattlesnake country, and they're pretty dangerous.

- Ooh ... they can give you a nasty bite!

- You can fly through the canyon in a helicopter or plane if you want. Are you going to do that?

English – Sprachkurs 2

- Yeah, we might do that later. I wouldn't mind trying a little white water rafting, too.
- Yeah, if you like getting wet you can take a raft down the Colorado River.
- I've never been on the rapids before. It's going to be quite an experience.
- Try not to fall in! Come on.

to found sth: etw. gründen
ever since: seitdem
to get tired of sth: einer Sache überdrüssig werden
scenery: Landschaft
to admire sth: etw. bestaunen
drawback: Nachteil
sprained ankle: verstauchter Knöchel
rattlesnake: Klapperschlange
rapids: Stromschnellen

7 San Francisco | Chinatown

Liang wird 30 und überlegt, wie und wo er den Geburtstag mit Familie und Freunden feiern wird. Damit sich niemand benachteiligt fühlt, müssen natürlich alle eingeladen werden. Aber vielleicht bekommt er bei Wong Chang Shuen einen Rabatt ...

- What am I going to do for my birthday?
- What do you want to do, Liang?
- Well, I think I'd like to take everybody to a restaurant.
- And just invite friends?
- No, I'd like my family to be there, too.
- You're planning something pretty big then?
- It's my thirtieth birthday. That's important enough, don't you think?
- Well, if you think it's something worth celebrating!
- And I want to announce my engagement at the party, too, for those who don't already know.
- And give it an official touch.
- How many people are going to be there?

- 🟥 About fifty, which is more than the last party and more than I can really afford, I guess.
- 🟨 But isn't that the tradition?
- 🟥 Yes, and I think it'll be really nice.
- 🟨 Sure it will, with all your friends and family all together in one place.
- 🟥 But that's what worries me.
- 🟨 What do you mean?
- 🟥 Well, there are some aunts and uncles I'll have to invite if the rest of the family is there.
- 🟨 You can't avoid that at these special celebrations.
- 🟥 But they always wear you down and talk about the stupidest things for hours.
- 🟨 I know, mine are the same.
- 🟥 And do they make a real fuss about everything, too?
- 🟨 No, it's my mother who's like that.
- 🟥 Really? Oh, my mother just keeps telling me what to do all the time.
- 🟨 And she'll still be doing that when you're forty and have four kids.
- 🟥 But I don't really mind. Anyway, where can I have the party?
- 🟨 Why don't you have it at Wong Chang Shuen's?
- 🟥 Ah yes! They make an excellent dim sum, and all sorts of special dishes.
- 🟨 Yeah, anything you can think of and really good. But it's going to cost even more than you thought.
- 🟥 But dad knows the owner, so I might get a good price.
- 🟨 Like for the Chinese New Year's celebrations last year.
- 🟥 The owner knew the guy who made all the dragons and told him everything at the restaurant that week was half price.
- 🟥 Maybe he hoped doing somebody a favor would give him a little bit of good luck for the New Year!

---

to invite: einladen
to celebrate: feiern
to announce sth: etw. bekannt geben
engagement: Verlobung
to afford sth: sich etw. leisten
to worry sb: jmdn. beunruhigen
to wear sb down: jmdn. fertig machen
to make a fuss about sth: um etw. viel Aufhebens machen
dragon: Drache

San Francisco | Golden Gate Bridge

Harry und Sally treffen sich auf der Golden Gate Bridge. Harry wurde gerade von seiner Freundin verlassen und Sally spendet ihm Trost. Wird aus dieser Freundschaft mehr?

- Hi! Sorry I'm late.
- Don't worry, I've just arrived too.
- Here are the papers you asked for.
- Thanks. How's your husband, and the kids of course?
- Oh they're doing fine. Paul's going to high school next month, provided everything goes according to plan.
- Good to hear that. Can't say the same for myself though.
- Are you still unhappy about Karen leaving you?
- Yeah, I guess it will take some time for me to get over it.
- Well try not to get too depressed about it.
- Well I know I can count on you if I need to talk about it.
- Sure, I'm always there to listen to you and give you advice, for what that's worth!
- It sure helps me, and I know you understand. Anyway, it's not that bad, I'm not going to jump off the bridge.
- They say the Golden Gate Bridge was always a favorite place for people to commit suicide, don't they?
- Ha! Yeah, but I think they try to prevent people from jumping off now.
- It baffles me why they should want to throw themselves off it. It's too beautiful to leave behind!
- It sure is nice, isn't it?
- It was built in the 30's by Joseph B. Straus.
- Isn't it the longest or highest suspension bridge in the world or something?
- No idea. It probably was at some point anyway.

English – Sprachkurs 2

- What's amazing is that it should stand up to earthquakes and hurricanes and things so long.

- Don't you think they could know about all that in the thirties?

- Well maybe with experience and modern technology it's easier to build big things nowadays.

- I guess so.

- Coming back to partnerships, maybe we should try it together.

- Hey, I'm a married woman and I want to keep it that way!

- I know, just kidding!

- We would make a great couple though, I admit that!

---

according to plan: nach Plan
to leave sb: jmdn. verlassen
to get over sth: über etw. hinwegkommen
advice: Rat
to commit suicide: Selbstmord begehen
to prevent sb from doing sth: jmdn. daran hindern, etw. zu tun
to baffle sb: jmdn. verblüffen
suspension bridge: Hängebrücke
earthquake: Erdbeben
to admit sth: etw. zugeben

---

9 San Francisco | An argument

Beim Einkaufen in San Francisco haben Vic und Claire ein typisches Gespräch unter Eheleuten. Eine harmlos begonnene Diskussion wird schnell zu einem Streit. Ist die Lage wirklich so brenzlig, wie es scheint?

- Come on, hurry up, can't you walk a bit faster?

- It's these shoes, they hurt after a while.

- Well why don't you buy shoes that fit and are comfortable?

- Will you just stop yelling at me?

- But we'll never get there on time if you walk like a snail!

- 🟨 Oh, shut up! It's my fault now is it? Who were we waiting for the whole time this morning?
- 🟥 You're the one who took ages in the shower.
- 🟨 But we wanted to leave at quarter after nine and I was ready.
- 🟥 So was I!
- 🟨 Oh bull! You were still standing there in your underpants!
- 🟥 Don't get hysterical.
- 🟨 I'm not getting hysterical! Why is it whenever I raise my voice, which is only rarely, you say I get hysterical just because I'm a woman? You're the one who keeps shouting at the top of your voice all the time!
- 🟥 Well I have every reason to. I did the shopping and cleared up the apartment while you were out having fun half the night with that Ronald friend of yours!
- 🟥 So that's what this is all about, you're just jealous! Well I always clear up the mess you leave so I think it's about time you did it for once!
- 🟥 That's not the point. You could have invited me to come out with you.
- 🟨 I can go out on my own sometimes too, you know, I don't have to be shackled to you.
- 🟥 Shackled! That's a nice way of putting it. If you feel tied down, just leave! I'm not holding you back.
- 🟨 I just might! You've been acting abysmally lately.
- 🟥 You like him, don't you?
- 🟨 Well yes, actually, quite honestly, I do, so be careful.
- 🟥 Well have a nice life with him! Or were you only planning on enjoying his attentions for a year or so?
- 🟨 God, Vic, I'm not having an affair!
- 🟥 How should I know? What am I meant to believe?
- 🟨 Just cool down. I can't stand your jealous tantrums.
- 🟥 Alright, sorry, I don't want to spoil our day.
- 🟨 Maybe I should have worn the other shoes.

---

to yell at sb: jmdn. anschreien
snail: Schnecke
bull(shit): Blödsinn
to shout: brüllen
jealous: eifersüchtig
shackled: angekettet
abysmally: entsetzlich
tantrum: Wutanfall
to spoil sth: etw. verderben

10 Atlanta | Olympic Games

Zwei Freunde sind im Olympiastadion von Atlanta. Sie haben beide viel gesehen und tauschen sich darüber aus. Wie es wohl ist, auf dem Siegertreppchen zu stehen, mit einer Goldmedaille um den Hals und der Nationalhymne im Ohr?

- Did you watch all the events?

- What do you mean all the events? You can't watch everything! But I saw most of the swimming events and track and field, and a little bit of virtually everything else.

- I watched all the races, of course: the one hundred and two hundred metre sprints are the classics. You can't miss them. And the hurdles, the relays ...

- Michael Johnson was amazing, wasn't he?

- Yeah. I must have seen those races and other Olympic highlights about ten times over.

- That's no problem with action replays in slow motion and close-up shots of all the competitors.

- Just imagine how happy and proud you must feel up there on the podium with a gold medal around your neck and the national anthem playing.

- Especially after all the effort you put in it, the pain and the strain, the years of tough training.

- Well, there are loads of other competitions you can win as well.

- Yes, but this one is probably the most prestigious.

- The most important thing is taking part, in regard to the spirit of the Olympic Games.

- But winning a medal, a gold one at that, is the best reward possible.

- It's a shame the atmosphere of the games was spoiled by the bombs.

- Yeah, that was a real shame. Fireworks are better!

- I hope bombs like those or the one in Oklahoma won't become part of normal everyday life in America.

🟨 No, I don't think so.

🟥 Anyway, there's not much likelihood of getting blown up yourself, is there?

🟨 No, that's true. By the way, do you still watch sports as much as you used to?

🟥 Yeah, I love it, baseball, rowing, volleyball, swimming, you name it, I watch it!

🟨 Are you hooked on sports or something?

🟥 In a way I guess I am, and I like keeping fit and active myself, and using my muscles a bit, but my weight won't let me. The first time you do something you feel exhausted, but the second time you're just tired!

🟨 Yeah, I think I should do more, like go jogging or something.

🟥 Jogging's boring! But it's all a matter of taste.

🟨 I prefer team games and ball games, football, tennis, squash ...

🟥 It's more social and you have the incentive to win.

🟨 Like the gold medal and the fame and glory at the Olympics.

🟥 Well, I wouldn't compare it to that!

🟨 Maybe not. I was pleased the States got the most medals though.

🟥 China, Germany and France did well, but Britain was way down on the list!

🟨 Yeah, but as we said, it's participating that counts.

🟥 Yeah yeah ...

---

event: Wettkampf
track and field: Leichtathletik
hurdles: Hürdenlauf
relay: Staffellauf
competitor: Teilnehmer
national anthem: Nationalhymne
strain: Belastung
reward: Belohnung
atmosphere: Stimmung
likelihood: Wahrscheinlichkeit
to be hooked on sth: nach etw. süchtig sein
exhausted: erschöpft
matter of taste: Geschmackssache
incentive: Anreiz
glory: Ruhm

11 Atlanta | Shopping mall

Ann und Todd sind im Einkaufszentrum und überlegen, was sie alles kaufen wollen. Todd möchte sich Elektrogeräte ansehen und Ann Dessous. Nach langem Verhandeln kann es dann endlich losgehen.

- I love the shopping mall! You can get just about everything here.

- Yeah, but I don't like being indoors all the time. Wouldn't you rather go shopping outside in the sunshine and fresh air?

- No! I don't want to catch a cold!

- Oh, that's a bunch of baloney! It's a beautiful day out there. It is warm, the sun is shining and the birds are singing. Don't you think that would be much nicer?

- No way, Todd! First of all it's hot as hell out there, and secondly you never know when the weather could change. We could get stuck in a thunderstorm! It's nice and air-conditioned in here, with light relaxing music in the background. Besides, just think of what would happen if all my bags and new clothes got wet!

- Yeah, you'd probably be an even bigger pain!

- Hey, now! Don't be a baby!

- Okay, okay, we're here now … so what else do you want to get?

- Ooh! You know that really trendy shoe store is having a close-out sale this week. Why don't we go take a look.

- Shoes? Ann, are you kidding? Our closet is already crammed with thousands of pairs of shoes. I really want to go to Sharper Image. They've got all the latest electronics and household appliances. It's a real shoppers paradise!

- Todd, you really have to buy some new shoes. These ones you have are starting to look a bit worn. And then we can go to Sharper Image, although I'm not sure if we can really afford a new stereo.

- Well, I never said I wanted to buy a new stereo. I'd just like to look around for a few minutes.

- Alright, that's fine. But if I go there with you, you have to come to Victoria's Secret with me. Maybe I'll buy some sexy lingerie.

- You want me to go to the underwear store with you? Ann, what if somebody sees me?

- Don't be silly, Todd. First of all it's not underwear, it's lingerie. Besides that, it'll be fun!

- Well, maybe I could help you find something special! But let's go to the CD store then, okay?

- Sure. We can look for those CDs you wanted.

- Excellent! There's a music store on the next floor.

- We could use some good new CDs for our party next Saturday.

- And then we can stop by Macy's on the second floor.

- Yeah, you definitely need a new suit for work, the old one is starting to look a little shabby.

- Actually, I was thinking of something a bit more flamboyant for the party. Maybe a trendy new suit, and a bright red tie!

- Todd, we're having a party, not a fashion show! Let's just look to see if we can find a few nice things to wear.

- Oh, Ann don't be such a party pooper! At work I have to wear the same things day in, day out, and on weekends I always wear jeans.

- Well, that doesn't mean you have to look like a clown when we have a party. Or do you want me to pretend I don't know you?

- Look, Ann, I just want to wear something different for a change!

- Okay, okay, I'm just kidding. I'll help you find something respectable, alright?

- Great! Now, why don't you let me help you with those bags?

---

shopping mall: Einkaufszentrum
bunch of baloney: Quatsch
pain: Nervensäge
crammed: vollgestopft
worn: abgelaufen
lingerie: Dessous
shabby: abgetragen
flamboyant: extravagant
party pooper: Partymuffel
for a change: zur Abwechslung
respectable: anständig

12 Atlanta | Airport

Zwei Reisende staunen über die Größe des Flughafens von Atlanta und das dortige Treiben. Der Flughafen ist einer der größten der Welt, und so gibt es viel zu beobachten, während sie auf ihren Flug warten.

- Atlanta International Airport is one of the busiest airports in the USA.

- Yeah, when I was here in December 1992, I heard over 42 million passengers a year check in here.

- And the number is probably much higher now.

- Look at them all. They're like ants!

- I really like airports and train stations with all the people coming and going.

- Yes, there's always a lot of activity, a lot to look at.

- You see all sorts of people, the most boring, the most beautiful and the weirdest.

- I mostly associate airports with work, so I don't get much pleasure out of traveling.

- Well, I go on business trips a lot too, but somehow the buzz of it still fascinates me.

- I do like it, but of course especially when I go on vacation. Which doesn't mean interesting things can't happen if you're on business.

- No, I flew to India and Thailand last year, and had to wait at the airport for about nine hours. They had canceled a flight because of technical problems, and delayed the others. It was absolute chaos, but I had time to read half a book and go through the duty-free shops three times.

- Didn't that really annoy you?

- Oh yes, it was a total waste of a day, but I killed a few hours reading an interesting novel. And I met a very nice woman who was a passenger on the same flight.

- Trust you to make time with a woman at the first opportunity!

- Oh, don't be stupid. She was just very nice. I certainly wouldn't have minded getting to know her much better.

English – Sprachkurs 2

- Was she on business, too?

- Yes, she works for our rival firm! Or was it our partner's?

- Well, if you're lucky, they'll headhunt you and then you can see her every day.

- Oh no, you don't want to be in each other's hair all day!

- But maybe you should have exchanged numbers.

- Yes, that would have been the best thing.

- Or arranged to meet up after landing at your destination. Oh well, you win some, you lose some!

- Well, it's a shame, but you don't have to make a mountain out of a molehill. We were both stuck in the same boat and that sort of binds you together.

- I agree. But next time you see her, don't forget to ask her for a date!

---

weird: seltsam
buzz: aufgeregtes Durcheinander
waste: Vergeudung
to exchange: austauschen
to make a mountain out of a molehill: aus einer Mücke einen Elefanten machen

---

13 Atlanta | Car rental

Ein Ehepaar möchte im Urlaub ein Auto mieten. Sie müssen sich für ein Auto entscheiden und die nötigen Unterlagen ausfüllen. Die Beratung des Vermieters ist wirklich umfassender als erwartet!

- Hello, we'd like to rent a car, please.

- For how long?

- For three days.

- How much does it cost?

- It depends on what car you take.

- Why, what types of car do you have to offer?

- You can have a normal four-door sedan, a pick-up truck, a station

English – Sprachkurs 2

wagon, a nice big Lincoln or Cadillac ... We have everything you need here.

■ We'll take the station wagon, please. We have two kids and lots of luggage, so it's more practical, and we're helping my brother transport something big later on, too.

■ OK, that'll cost you fifty dollars a day.

■ That's fine.

■ Can I see your driver's license please?

■ Here's mine.

■ And here's mine.

■ OK. And do you have a major credit card?

■ Here you are.

■ Thank you. Could you just fill out this form, please?

■ Certainly. Do you have a map of Atlanta and of the area?

■ Sure, and here's a small guide to good places to eat and the sights to see if you've never been here before.

■ Is there a restaurant you can recommend?

■ Well, personally, I like 'Pat's Revenge'. The food, the service, the atmosphere, everything is just wonderful.

■ Alright then, we'll make sure we don't miss out on that one.

■ It's worth reserving a few days in advance, and if you do go there, try the chicken wings and Pat's Spicy Special. It's awesome! And mighty hot!

■ Oh, I'm not too hot on very spicy dishes.

■ But I am! I think I'm going to love it.

■ Where is it, anyway?

■ It's downtown. You can't miss it. I'll circle it on the map for you.

■ That would be great, thanks.

■ I think it's in that guide, too, but if not, just ask anyone in the neighborhood. They'll be able to tell you the phone number or at least how to get there.

■ Thank you very much.

---

to rent a car: ein Auto mieten
sedan: Limousine
station wagon: Kombi
driver's license: Führerschein
map: Stadtplan
to recommend: empfehlen
revenge: Rache
it's worth: es lohnt sich
to be hot on sth: etw. gern mögen
downtown: Stadtmitte
neighborhood: nähere Umgebung

4 Chicago | Art Institute

Zwei kulturinteressierte Frauen treffen sich im Art Institute in Chicago. An diesem Ort muss man sich natürlich über Malerei und diverse Künstler unterhalten.

- Monet, Gauguin, Cézanne, Degas, they're all here.

- Yes, Renoir, Van Gogh ... They have quite a collection!

- I love the Impressionists. They had a really fresh, lively, colorful way of painting.

- I like all sorts of paintings, belonging to all the movements. Even the very old ones.

- So do I really. They all have their appeal. But I think the Impressionists are my favorite painters.

- You can get a bit too much of them though. Just about every office has a reproduction of a Van Gogh or Cézanne.

- Or of Monet's 'Waterlilies' for example.

- Yes. I think the original of that is at the National Gallery in London.

- Well especially for an office, you can't really go wrong with the Impressionists. They're mostly pleasant, with lots of light, and no naked bodies to distract you while you're working!

- Except some of Renoir's works of course.

- It's funny that the Art Institute of Chicago should have so many nice paintings.

- In my opinion, it's good to have famous works of art dispersed all over the world. Like that, all the major museums have some to display and people everywhere can admire them.

- There's more to see in Chicago itself. Works by Picasso, or Chagall.

- There's a mosaic by Chagall called 'The Four Seasons'.

- Yes, you have to go to the square in front of the First National Bank building.

- Did you know that there was so much art to see in this city?

- Of course. As far as architecture is concerned, it's quite interesting, too.

- Yeah there are some pretty nice modern buildings, the Sears Tower and the Atrium Mall in the State of Illinois Center.

- And if you're interested in architecture, the Frank Lloyd Wright buildings are a must, in the Astor Street District, or the Robie House, which is quite well-known.

- Anyway, I've seen enough paintings here now. You can't take in too much in one go.

- Alright, let's go and have a bite to eat somewhere.

- And sit down and rest our legs. We've been walking around the city and the museum non-stop for four hours!

---

painting: Gemälde
movement: Bewegung
appeal: Reiz
pleasant: hübsch
dispersed: verstreut
to display sth: etw. ausstellen
to admire sth: etw. bewundern
to take sth in: etw. aufnehmen

5 Chicago | Symphony Orchestra

Chicago hat eines der berühmtesten Sinfonieorchester Amerikas. Zwei Musikerinnen unterhalten sich über ihre Arbeit und ihre Liebe zur Musik.

- We can count ourselves lucky, really, to be able to play in the Chicago Symphony Orchestra.

- When you think about it, there are loads of aspiring violinists who would love to play here.

- And there's a lot of young talent around.

- It won't be long before a couple of the budding violinists we see now are playing in the orchestra here.

- No. I saw a few excellent players at various recitals and competitions.

- They all dream of a solo career or a position as first violinist in Chicago, L.A. or New York.

- Some are technically very good, but too young. Somehow the way they play lacks inspiration and interpretation.

- Yeah, I guess that comes with age, to some extent. We'll learn a lot with time, too. Would you prefer to be a soloist?

- Yes, I would really. But you've got to be tough for that, I think.

- My dream is to follow in the footsteps of Heifetz, Menuhin, Stern or Perlman.

- Playing Mendelssohn's Violin Concerto at Carnegie Hall, for example. That'd be the pinnacle of any violinist's career. But I'm quite happy here in the orchestra, too.

- Yes, I like the atmosphere among the musicians and playing in front of a full audience.

- And some conductors develop a special rapport with the orchestra.

- What are the highlights which you have had in your working life so far?

- Well, I remember one fantastic night a few years ago, James Levine was conducting, and there were many famous people in the audience.

■ And did you play well?

■ Yes, of course, but that's not all. A friend of mine who was in the audience came up to me in the intermission to announce the birth of my little niece!

■ That's great! And does she enjoy music?

■ Of course. And she's called Maria after Maria Callas. Anyway, let's get going.

■ Yeah. Back to work. We're having a full general rehearsal tomorrow, and I think it'll all go well. But I feel pretty tired today, so I'm going to go to bed early.

■ So am I. It's been a tiring week.

---

aspiring: aufstrebend
budding: angehend
recital: Konzert
to some extent: in gewissem Maße
pinnacle: Höhepunkt
conductor: Dirigent
intermission: Pause
rehearsal: Probe

16 Chicago | Futures market

Aktien, Investmentfonds, Warentermingeschäfte ... an der Börse in Chicago ist es manchmal sehr hektisch. Zwei Börsenmakler machen eine kleine Pause und unterhalten sich über ihre Arbeit. Sie haben es wirklich nicht leicht!

■ Friday was a little bit calmer than Thursday morning. All hell broke loose on the trading floor.

■ I think all the markets were going wild.

■ I asked John what it was like. He said he had McMahon shouting 'Where's gold? Where's gold?' on the phone.

■ Yeah, and he's the sort of guy who wouldn't raise an eyebrow if I stripped in front of him.

■ It was certainly frantic on our commodities futures.

- From corn to pork bellies to currencies, everything was going crazy.
- I was transacting around ten trades a minute, calls and puts on futures contracts no end.
- Days like that can take a few years off your life.
- Yeah, well at least it's not like that all the time.
- By the way, how long have you been in the business?
- Let me see, six years here and then a stint in Frankfurt and London and then back here ... about 18 years.
- God, so long! I joined Financial Futures straight after college. That makes just five and a half years. I don't think I could take it for eighteen.
- Well, with the current spell of firing, you might not have to!
- Oh, it's alright. They're not letting people go like three years ago. So what college did you go to?
- I didn't. You don't have to study anything to do my job. You just have to think quickly, to be the right kind of man for the job.
- Or woman.

---

trading floor: Börsenparkett
to raise an eyebrow: mit der Wimper zucken
frantic: hektisch
commodities futures: Warenterminbörse
to transact: eine Transaktion vornehmen
calls and puts: Kaufs- und Verkaufsoptionen
stint: Weile
spell: Zeit
to fire sb: jmdn. feuern
to let sb go: jmdn. entlassen

17 Washington | World Bank

In Washington D.C. ist die Zentrale der Weltbank. Bill und Ted unterhalten sich über die Funktion und Aufgabe dieser Einrichtung. Sind die Freunde politisch derselben Meinung?

- I guess lots of people work for the government in Washington, hey?

- Apparently, around three hundred and fifty thousand people work in administration, and tens of thousands in the various national and international organizations.

- Yeah, the World Bank and the International Monetary Fund are based here, for example.

- That's the World Bank building there, I think. What does it do exactly?

- Well, it aims to promote reconstruction and development and raise the standard of living.

- In underdeveloped countries you mean?

- Yes, and anywhere else where it's needed.

- And it helps them by granting loans?

- Yes, under certain conditions like improving the rate of tax collection. And the IMF promotes international cooperation on monetary policies, amongst other things. It supports member states with difficulties in their balance of payments by giving them short-term loans.

- And what do the members do or promise to do in return?

- Well, for instance, they ensure the continuing stability of their currency and don't just change its value at will.

- I suppose it's a way of applying pressure on unstable or volatile countries and keeping countries together.

- Like GATT, during the Uruguay round of talks for example. It all helps to prevent trade wars and to bring down trade barriers.

English – Sprachkurs 2

- I'll just take your word for it. I didn't study politics and economics.
- Would you like to be a politician?
- Nothing less than the President himself!
- Really?
- Don't be stupid!
- I'd prefer it to being a peanut farmer or an actor!
- The money's alright, but not the responsibility that comes with all that power!
- And being hounded and scrutinized by journalists doesn't sound wonderful.
- No, it's not exactly my idea of a relaxing working life!
- I mean, sure, meeting all the top guys from all the countries, that must be real interesting.
- And working here every day. Capitol Hill and the White House are mighty impressive.
- But I couldn't get used to sleeping only a few hours a night.
- And I'd have absolutely no idea of how to run a country and what to do.
- Neither would I, really. But it's up to them, it's what they're paid for.
- Paid a lot for!

---

administration: Verwaltung
reconstruction: Wiederaufbau
underdeveloped countries: Entwicklungsländer
to grant: gewähren
loan: Kredit
monetary policy: Währungspolitik
short-term: kurzfristig
volatile: instabil
to hound sb: jmdn. jagen
to scrutinize sb: jmdn. abschätzig mustern
to run a country: einen Staat verwalten

18 Washington | Hospital

Im Krankenhaus zu arbeiten ist nicht leicht. Diese zwei Krankenschwestern in Washington D.C. sind wirklich erschöpft. Sie beschweren sich zwar ein bisschen über die Arbeit, aber die Patienten liegen ihnen trotzdem sehr am Herzen.

■ I'm certainly busy, you can say that again! Man, I hardly get a minute's rest!

■ Yes, it's hard work. You're on your feet all day and have to turn patients over and lift them up.

■ Sure, and you work long hours, with night shifts and all. It's damned tiring.

■ The doctors work overtime, there aren't enough nurses, there aren't enough beds.

■ Sometimes I'm so worn out I just feel like lying down on one of these beds and sleeping for ten hours!

■ And who's going to look after all the patients? And I'm sure they want you to take care of them just as much as they want me to.

■ How is Mr Cartwright feeling today?

■ Not too bad. He's glad the operation's over.

■ The doctor's going to come around this afternoon to have another look at him.

■ But it won't be necessary to operate again, will it?

■ No, it was quite straightforward. There were no complications. One time under anesthetic and one operation are enough, and not too many shots and medicine!

■ He'll probably be out of the hospital in two days - and I have to go on working now.

---

rest: Ruhe
night shift: Nachtschicht
to work overtime: Überstunden machen
worn out: erschöpft
under anesthetic: unter Narkose
shot: Spritze

English – Sprachkurs 2

19 Washington | At the hairdresser's

Lolas Haare müssen wieder in Form gebracht werden, und dafür hat sie scheinbar den richtigen **Friseur** gefunden. Er macht alles genau, wie sie es beschreibt. Leider redet er ein bisschen zu viel!

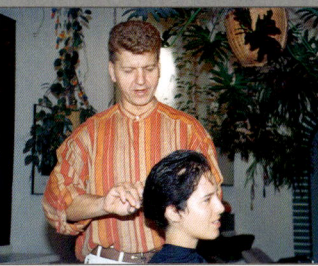

- Can I bring you a coffee or a magazine?

- No coffee, thanks, I've just had two, but I'll have the magazine please.

- Sure, here you are. And if you could sit over here ... How would you like it done?

- Um, shortish at the sides and at the back, please. I mean, nicely trimmed.

- And how much do you want off the top?

- Oh, not too much.

- Like that?

- Yes, that's fine, thanks. It's especially the hair on my neck which was getting on my nerves. I don't like it when it gets too long.

- When did you last have your hair cut?

- Oh, ages ago. I can't remember when exactly, actually. Although I actually quite like it, because you can sit and rest and let your thoughts wander.

- And think, and solve a problem, or make a decision about something you weren't sure about.

- Yes, last time I decided not to have my car repaired, but to sell what was left of it and buy a new one.

- Did you have an accident with it?

- Yes, it was almost a write-off.

- Is that alright like that?

- Fine. You can even take a tiny bit more off.

- Excuse me for a second. I just have to arrange an appointment with the customer here. Right, I'm back. Sorry about that.

- Don't worry about it.

- Don't you have to go to work today?

🟨 No, I'm on vacation for a couple of days. I come from New York. I'm just passing through here. I'm staying at a friend's place before I move on to Richmond to visit some other friends.

🟥 Oh, I spent four years in New York. That's where I learned all about hairdressing. I used to work somewhere where they did the latest styles right away, as soon as they were in fashion. We always had to stay on the ball in that respect. I really liked it there and I made a lot of friends. I think it would be great to have some friends in lots of countries and big cities. So you could stay everywhere for free as well as see old friends. Of course, it's not quite as easy if you're married with kids. Are you married?

🟨 No, I'm single. Do you always talk so much with your customers?

---

to trim: (Haare) schneiden
off the top: oben abgeschnitten
to let one's thoughts wander: seinen Gedanken freien Lauf lassen
write-off: Totalschaden
a tiny bit: ein klein bisschen
to stay on the ball: am Ball bleiben

---

20 Orlando | Gossip on the beach

Martin hat seinen Kumpel Roger an den Strand direkt vor seiner Haustür eingeladen. Roger ist begeistert, während Martin, als Rettungsschwimmer, auch die Gefahren des Meeres kennt.

🟨 Wow, this is great that you have a house right here on the beach! I wish I could come here every day!

🟥 Yeah, but when you live here you have to put up with a lot of people, like that guy, who like to show off! But I'm a lifeguard and being on the beach every day is pretty hard work! And you have to put up with a lot of hassle.

🟨 At least you get to spend a lot of time working on your tan! And I can tell by the glint in your eye that you love your job!

- Well I do like the work, but sometimes it's hard to get by on the small salary they give me. And it's pretty dangerous out there!
- Look at that beautiful beach and the clear water ... how can it be dangerous?
- Well, first of all, it really gets on your nerves when you have to stare at that beautiful clear water all day long and besides that, the water isn't as safe as it looks!
- What? Are you afraid of being eaten by a shark? Or are you worried about being attacked by a horde of jellyfish?
- C'mon ... you know that we hardly have any shark attacks and that the jellyfish on our beaches are relatively harmless.
- Then I don't get what's so dangerous about being a lifeguard.
- You can't really see it, but there is a very strong current in the water. At low tide, it can drag you almost a mile out into the ocean. Most people can't swim back.
- Yikes! That does sound a little scary!
- Yeah it is! But you do get training on how to handle the situation. I've been a lifeguard for six years now, and I really take my job seriously. I've also had training in scuba diving, in case there is a diving accident.
- Wow! I wish I had more time for things like that, but when I go to the beach I usually just have my towel and my trunks. Do you get along with your boss and your co-workers?
- We all get along great, but it isn't like Baywatch here! Sometimes the other lifeguards do get on my nerves a little bit. You also have to stay in top condition all the time. If you put on any weight, it could slow you down in an emergency.
- I guess you have to put off your vacation too, don't you? If your job is about laying around on the beach, who needs a vacation?
- Hey! I don't have to put up with your jokes all the time, do I? You should try to get it into your head that we all work pretty hard here!
- Okay, okay, I'm sorry! It could be me who you drag out of the water one day.
- But even though I just lay around on the beach all summer, I do like to go on vacation!
- So do you like to go someplace nice and cold to relax?
- No way! It would really get on my nerves to get stuck in some cold, dark place for a few weeks. I need the sun, baby! Since I have to take vacation

when it's winter here, I usually go to Australia where it's summer, or to Hawaii where it's always summer!

■ Australia, Hawaii ... it sounds like you're an avid surfer too!

■ You bet! If somebody gets in trouble further out in the water, we use a surfboard to go out to help them.

■ So you surf out to save them?

■ Not really. We paddle out on the board, and then use it to bring the person back. Sometimes it is pretty frightening out there, but I love the work, and I love the beach!

■ No matter what, I still wish I could come to the beach every day!

---

to put up with: auskommen mit
hassle: Mühe
glint: Glitzern
jellyfish: Qualle
to get sth: etw. kapieren
current: Strömung
low tide: niedriger Wasserstand
trunks: Badehose
avid: eifrig

21 Orlando | Fast-food restaurant

Mikey lädt Lisa zum Essen ein. Es ist ihre erste Verabredung und Mikey hat Romantisches im Sinn. Wird etwas daraus?

■ You just wait here, I'll get the food.

■ I can come with you to help you carry it all if you want.

■ No, it's alright, I'll manage.

■ Well, you only have two hands. Let me help you carry it to the table.

■ No, you wait here, while I get our order.

■ Well, let me at least give you some money.

■ No, out the money away. I want to invite you. It's my treat! Now, what would you like?

- I'll have a cheeseburger with a large order of fries, please.
- And what would you like to drink?
- A diet coke please. Don't forget the ketchup, Mikey!
- Of course not. I'll be right back with your order.
- Wow! What service! You should be a waiter.
- Only the best for you my dear.
- Ooh. The service is not only good looking but also friendly. This is better than a real restaurant!
- Well, this is a special day. This is our first date, after all.
- I just hope you remember that good girls don't kiss on the first date!
- The thought never entered my mind. I'm just a friendly sort of guy, that's all.
- This burger looks good, and it smells good. Now, let's see if it tastes good.
- I just love fast food. I think it's better than anything a real restaurant has to offer.
- Yeah, I pretty much like it all, whether its burgers, fried chicken or donuts and bagels.
- I'm not picky either. I'll eat anything on the menu.
- I'll eat just about anything too, but I'm not too crazy about seafood. What about you?
- Well, I like salmon and other kinds of fish, but I don't really like lobster or crab.
- And don't forget that seafood gives you bad breath, too. If you have bad breath nobody will want to kiss you!
- But these French fries won't give me bad breath, will they?
- Maybe you should just concentrate on eating your food for now. We'll see what happens later.
- I have to admit, it's hard to concentrate on food, when I have such enchanting company.
- Flattery will get you nowhere. Now give me some of your chicken!
- Hey, this is mine! Eat yours first.
- Oh yeah? No chicken, then no kiss!
- Well, can I at least have your phone number?

---

to manage: zurechtkommen
The thought never entered my mind.:
Das ist mir nie in den Sinn gekommen.
picky: wählerisch
salmon: Lachs
lobster: Hummer
bad breath: schlechter Atem
enchanting: bezaubernd
flattery: Schmeicheleien

22 Orlando | Cape Canaveral

Zwei Touristen besuchen Cape Canaveral, den Stützpunkt der amerikanischen Weltraumfähren. Sie bewundern den technischen Fortschritt und unterhalten sich über den Nutzen der Raumfahrt. Wollen sie auch Astronauten werden?

- I must admit, I don't care about space and all that very much.
- Well, it's fascinating to see all these rockets.
- Yeah, just think of all the money and effort that has been put into the development of all the technology here.
- I wonder how different our idea of the world would be if we didn't know about space and all the planets.
- Or if Apollo 11 hadn't been sent to the moon in '69.
- At the time when such projects were being planned, I bet people thought they were impossible or it was sheer madness. But look at the advantages now of having satellites and the knowledge of our solar system.
- Call it science or just curiosity - research has led to much progress in the world.
- And to a lot of bad things.
- We can do without space and rockets as far as I'm concerned.
- I guess so. Would you go up into space in the shuttle if you had the chance?
- What, if I was an astronaut you mean?
- Or if it was possible for normal people to travel regularly and easily to space and back. In fifty years, say.
- I'll be gone in fifty years, and without having missed anything.
- But wouldn't you want to, for the experience?
- You must be joking! No, I like it down here on Earth, thank you.

---

effort: Mühe
solar system: Sonnensystem
curiosity: Neugierde
research: Forschung
as far as I'm concerned: was mich betrifft
shuttle: Raumfähre

English – Sprachkurs 2

New York | Little Italy

Max und sein Freund Richie treffen Maria in Little Italy im Herzen von New York City. Sie sind überzeugte New Yorker und erzählen, was in der Stadt alles los ist. Ihr Magen knurrt – wo gehen sie jetzt hin?

- Chelsea and Soho – this is the heart of New York's art world.

- Yes, I went to a very interesting exhibition of paintings in Chelsea the other day.

- Where was it?

- It was at the artist's private home. Quite small – there must have been only about fifty people in all there that afternoon. It was nice and personal. You could have a chat with the artist himself and talk to many other people over a glass of Buck's Fizz.

- Oh, refreshments were served, too? That's nice. There are always a great deal of cultural events happening in New York – exhibitions and concerts, and often outdoors in Chelsea or Soho.

- Yeah, people perform acrobatic tricks and play music in Washington Square.

- I listened to a short open-air concert in Battery Park during my lunch hour two days ago. I think it was organized by the borough.

- I regret not doing more, though. There is so much going on in New York, but you never seem to get around to making the most of what's on offer.

- I know where we can go for lunch today. I know a nice little restaurant in Little Italy.

- What's it called?

- Well, I ran into James in Little Italy two weeks ago and he recommended this restaurant to me. I'm afraid I can't recall the name of it, but I'm sure I can find it again without any problem.

- Well, you lead the way. I'll just have to trust you!

- Ciao Maria, how are you doing?

- Hi! I'm fine. Are you coming to Giovanni's for lunch?

- We weren't going to, but it doesn't matter.

- My brother and I are preparing for la festa di San Gennaro the day after tomorrow.

- Oh, yeah, I'm looking forward to all that great food. Are you doing anything special at the restaurant?

- Sure. There's a special menu all day and a party in the evening with delicious Italian specialties and free house wine. Are you coming?

- Yeah, you can count on me. And you, Richie?

- I don't know. I was going to see if I could get tickets for a musical.

- Oh, you can go to musicals all year! Come along.

- Be there or be square!

- Alright. You didn't have to twist my arm much, did you?

Buck's Fizz: Sekt mit Orangensaft
exhibition: Ausstellung
borough: Verwaltungsbezirk
to make the most of sth: das Beste aus etw. machen
to run into sb: jmdm. über den Weg laufen
to twist sb's arm: jmdn. zu etw. überreden

24 New York | Wall Street

Harry und Jake sind Börsenmakler an der Wall Street und haben viel zu tun. Doch in der Pause haben sie etwas anderes zu besprechen. Harry interessiert sich für seine Kollegin Marina - nicht nur aus geschäftlichen Gründen.

- Hey, I need to go up to the office in ten minutes.

- Why, you scared Max is going to fire you for having a half-hour lunch break?

English – Sprachkurs 2

- No, but it's the best time to catch Aaron and Sam before they go off.

- Yes, they always want information from you, but when you want to ask them something, they don't know or they don't have any time.

- Remember to phone Marina up later to catch up on the latest regarding the management buyout and the insider trading business.

- I'm making progress in other ways, too.

- What do you mean?

- I couldn't resist asking her out for dinner on Thursday. And she doesn't object to, uh, resuming business talks over a glass of wine next Thursday either.

- Hey, watch out! She's extremely attractive but her company's still our hottest competition.

- Yeah, and I know Max gets a bit touchy about such things.

- Look, I have to go back now. Can you buy me two of those sandwiches like the ones you got yesterday?

- Sure, Alex, I'll be up in fifteen minutes.

- What are you going to do?

- I think I'm just going to take a walk around Battery Park.

- Or you could go and see Mark at the NYSE. If you do, give him my regards and remind him to reply to John Goodridge in London a.s.a.p.

- That's not about the job at Goldman Sachs here in New York though, is it?

- No, no, it's just that we're planning to go to London in two weeks. You know, one hour's meeting as a pretext to spend four days including the weekend on the town.

- If it's anything like the last trip, you won't be fit till next month!

- Doesn't mean I can't work!

- Nothing wrong with clinching deals in a drunken stupor you mean?

- No, but momentary degeneracy has never hurt anyone!

- It just gives you all the more energy to get going afterwards.

- You certainly have to get going at our company. They make you work like mad here!

---

to resume sth: etw. wieder aufnehmen
touchy: empfindlich
regards: Grüße
pretext: Vorwand
to clinch a deal: ein Geschäft abschließen
degeneracy: schlechtes Benehmen

25 New York | 5th Avenue

Die feinen Damen von der 5th Avenue haben vielleicht Probleme! Das Hündchen mag seinen Lachs nicht, der richtige Pelzmantel ist nicht zu finden, und dieser Service bei Tiffany's ... !

- Fiffy's been acting a bit funny lately.
- Why's that?
- I don't know, but Robert says that maybe he needs company.
- Suggesting that you should get another little dog, so that Fiffy has a friend to play around with?
- Yes, but I think he would just like more different types of food, and something special to cheer him up now and again.
- Why don't you give him a dish with finely cut up salmon and steak and stuff?
- Yup, I'll give him that tonight.
- By the way, did you find that coat you wanted?
- Oh, I tried Bloomingdales and Macy's but what I saw wasn't quite right.
- By the look on your face that day, I ... I don't think there was anything which could have pleased you.
- I know, Robert often says I'm difficult to please.
- Well if I don't find what I need at Macy's or some other big store, I just drop in at some of the more exclusive places.
- Of course, you get better and more personal service.
- And some of the customers are quite prominent people. I'm sure I recognized Meryl Streep the other day.
- Hey, I saw a delightful little brooch at Tiffany's the day before yesterday. It was simply fabulous!
- How much did it cost?
- Well it cost twenty five thousand dollars, but I really need another

English – Sprachkurs 2

brooch or necklace. And it's just the right thing, with five diamonds on it.

- But not too flashy I hope.
- Oh no, really quite decent, and Robert says that at that price it's quite a good buy.
- Well I've set my heart on a beautiful red dress which they have on display at Goodley's at the moment. It's excellent quality and smart but also really tight and sexy, and they have it in blue as well in case red's too visible.
- At your age you can afford to wear things like that.
- Oh you can't imagine how difficult it is keeping in shape. I work out at the studio two times a week to keep my butt and my legs firm.
- Robert says I spend too much time in the bathroom putting on cleansing lotions and facial day creams. But I know what keeps my skin soft and looking healthy and I'm sure he prefers it too, really.
- You know at what tremendous speed your skin can become rough and not firm any more if you don't take care of it. Hey, do you want to go and have one of those delicious salads at that place on Lexington Avenue?
- OK, although Robert says there's a place ...
- Never mind what Robert says! We're going there!

---

funny: seltsam
to cheer sb up: jmdn. aufmuntern
to please sb: jmdm. gefallen
to drop in: vorbeischauen
delightful: entzückend
brooch: Brosche
to set one's heart on sth: sein Herz an etw. hängen
tight: eng
tremendous: ungeheuer

26 New York | Jewish synagogue

New York ist das Zentrum der Juden in den USA. Irma besucht seinen Freund Josh in New York und sie sprechen über die Juden in Amerika. Josh hätte gerne, dass Irma auch nach New York zieht. Vielleicht kann ihn ja das gute jüdische Essen locken.

- This is a beautiful synagogue, built in 1870. And has a wonderful example of a church or synagogue rose window. It's one of the largest rose windows in the world.

- How large is the Jewish community in New York?

- Oh, there are about 1.2 million Jews living in New York.

- Half my family lives here even though I don't myself.

- Why don't you come over and live here with us and your family?

- I can't really, I have my commitments where I am now, in London.

- Ah, where there's a will, there's a way!

- Sure, that's true, alright already. I'll think about it.

- I don't want to push you, but you know you'd like it.

- Of course I would, what do you think?

- Anyway, let's get some food.

- I'm starving.

- There's a great delicatessen further up the street.

- Talking about food, did I tell you we had twenty-two cookery books at home?

- It's not the number of books you have which makes you a good cook.

- No, but my wife is a marvelous cook. She uses the books to give her ideas, not to follow word for word.

- You enjoy good food, do you?

- You can't only eat matzos all year!

- I'll show you a few places where they sell excellent quality kosher food. They have an enormous range of products.

English – Sprachkurs 2

- And I'll do you something later on which you'll love. It's a little recipe I got from Rabbi Lionel Green at home.

- I'm looking forward to it. You can cook something every day during your stay if you want.

- Hey, don't ask for too much or you won't get anything!

rose window: Rosettenfenster
community: Gemeinde
commitment: Verpflichtungen
to push sb to do sth: jmdn. drängen, etw. zu tun
cookery book: Kochbuch
cook: Koch
marvelous: exzellent
matzo: Matzen (ungesäuertes Brot)

27 Los Angeles | In the office

Das Geschäft in Europa läuft nicht so gut wie gehofft. Der Vorstandsvorsitzende hält eine Besprechung ab, um eine Strategie für die Zukunft zu entwickeln. Vielleicht wäre es doch besser, eine Geschäftsstelle in Europa aufzumachen.

- I'd like to thank you for taking the time to meet with me today. We have a lot of important things to discuss. We've managed to secure our share of the market in Canada and sales have continued to grow in the U.S. but what worries me is how things are progressing in Europe. Now, I'd like to discuss how we can succeed in increasing our market share in Europe.

- I agree, but you have to bear in mind that we don't have a lot of experience in Europe.

- You have a point there.

- Quite frankly, you have to admit, that our products are the best on the market, and everyone knows that.

- I think you're right, Susan. If we had greater exposure, we could expand our market share.

English – Sprachkurs 2

- That's true to some extent, but there are other aspects to think about to avoid making mistakes.
- I would like to emphasize taking the trouble to maintain a high level of service!
- To be honest, we also need to assess our past performance.
- Well, we can't postpone doing this until later. We simply can't afford to risk losing more customers and contracts.
- Susan, don't be ridiculous. With talk like that, you'll manage to put everybody in a foul mood. You have to remember that we have succeeded in securing our share of the market in Canada.
- I'd like to emphasize that we took the trouble to focus on customer needs in Canada and it really paid off.
- I think we would be more effective if we centered our marketing efforts in Europe.
- Well, this has proven to be a successful solution in Canada. If we could use a similar model, we should be able to increase our market share. You have to bear in mind, though, that Europe is not Canada! Things could get tricky!
- I think we can succeed if we can manage to set up a marketing team in every individual country, and not have it all led by our offices here.
- We really should emphasize putting someone on site. If we had a marketing team on location, we would be more responsive to our customer needs.
- Yes, we currently only have one marketing office covering all of Europe. And that office is based here in Los Angeles. And I just don't think that it's effective.
- I think we have a lot to gain by expanding our European marketing operation.
- But wouldn't that cost a lot? Do you think we could afford investing the resources?
- Well, maybe. It might entail reducing the size of the American office to cut costs.
- Considering the travel costs involved, this could be viable option.
- A complete cost analysis is necessary before making a final decision.
- I'm afraid this won't be enough. Maybe we should also consider expanding the product line. Currently, we're only selling our most popular products in Europe.
- That's true. Market research has shown that there is a lot of

- opportunity for specialized products in Europe.
- And if we had a marketing team in Europe we would be able to tailor our products to our customer's needs.
- Yes, I think by introducing a broader product line, combined with establishing a marketing team based in Europe, we could turn things around.
- Yes, I think we should weigh the possibilities.
- Susan, why don't you organize a team to do some research to see if this is worthwhile.
- I'll get started on that right away.
- Great! I think this meeting was really worthwhile. We have come up with some excellent proposals and I'm looking forward to seeing your report.

(market) share: (Markt-)Anteil
to bear sth in mind: etw. beachten
exposure: Aufmerksamkeit
to emphasize: betonen
to maintain: aufrechterhalten
to assess: bewerten
to postpone sth: etw. verschieben
tricky: knifflig
responsive: entgegenkommend
to entail doing sth: es erforderlich machen, etw. zu tun
viable option: durchführbare Alternative

28 Los Angeles | Silicon Valley

Auf einer Computermesse unterhalten sich zwei Interessierte über die neuste Technologie und deren Auswirkung auf die Gesellschaft. Silicon Valley ist eindeutig das Herzstück der Computerindustrie.

- This is the heart of the computer industry.
- It's an important place for the United States.
- And for the whole world!
- Yes, in this age of telecommunications.

- ■ If you think about it, almost every office and every home has a computer, a fax, a telephone ...
- ■ Yeah, everyone's talking to everyone else at the same time all over the world.
- ■ A world with people linked up to the World Wide Web, surfing on the Internet, talking to people on the other side of the world.
- ■ Names like Microsoft, IBM, Apple, HP, Compaq, Intel, Motorola are household names in every country.
- ■ Are they taking over our lives?
- ■ Well, so many things depend on computers nowadays.
- ■ We can't really do without them, I agree.
- ■ And why should we? They make things much easier and better and faster.
- ■ And you can be hundreds of times more creative with them.
- ■ And calculate anything more quickly and accurately and store much more.
- ■ I'm just thinking of all the people who have trouble understanding how they work.
- ■ But it's always been like that with new things, especially if you didn't grow up with them.
- ■ I'm in the business, and even I have trouble sometimes keeping up with the innovations and new technology.

---

age: Zeitalter
linked up: vernetzt
to depend on: abhängen von
to grow up with sth: mit etw. aufwachsen
to keep up with sth: mit etw. Schritt halten
innovation: Neuerung

Los Angeles | Rodeo Drive

Alan und seine Freundin sind auf der Suche nach schicker Kleidung. Auf dem Rodeo Drive sind sie genau richtig, eine bessere Auswahl findet man kaum. Sie überlegen, was sie aneinander mögen.

- There must be loads of stores down on Rodeo Drive where I can get a suitable snazzy outfit for the celebration.

- I know you're going to look around for ages and you're going to go home with nothing in your hands.

- Well I just hate trying on clothes for hours and they're not my size or not good quality or look stupid.

- I tell you what, go wearing just a long tie. That would be different.

- Yeah, and everyone can have a good laugh at me.

- Well you have to attract attention to yourself somehow.

- I can't imagine how you manage to get all the attention.

- It's because I'm bubbly, open, witty and friendly, and I'm an understanding person, I can listen.

- The only thing is, I don't see when you get the chance to listen.

- Yeah, all right, I know I talk a lot too.

- I guess that's sometimes more tedious than shopping for clothes, right? Well I don't mind, quite the opposite.

- Better than dating someone who's a complete bore and says nothing!

- Like my last girlfriend. That was about as exciting as watching paint dry!

- What I like about you is that you're cool, calm and collected, and you have a great dry sense of humor. Anyway, go in there and buy yourself a nice jacket.

- Why don't we just go for dinner instead? Since I'm not buying anything, I can pay for it. We can be at Rizzi's Wine Bar in half an hour. Does that sound good?

- Sure, sounds great, and with the saved money we just have time for you to buy me a ticket to the Bahamas on the way.

- How did you know I wanted to take you on a trip to the Bahamas?

- Because you're as white as a sheet and I need some blue water and white sand. And if you leave your planner lying around, what do you expect?

- It'll be a surprise for me if I ever get to surprise you!

---

snazzy: schick
to attract attention: Aufmerksamkeit erregen
bubbly: lebhaft
witty: geistreich
tedious: ermüdend
bore: Langweiler
sheet: Bettlaken
planner: Terminkalender